ADVANCED

Elvis

WITHDRAWN
COURSE

CACONRAD

soft skull press
brooklyn

Author photo Copyright © 2009 by Heather Raquel Phillips
www.heatherraquelphillips.com

Library of Congress Cataloging-in-Publication Data is available.

ISBN 978-1-59376-243-8

Cover design by Goodloe Byron
Interior design by Neuwirth Associates
Printed in the United States of America

Soft Skull Press
An Imprint of Counterpoint LLC
2117 Fourth Street
Suite D
Berkeley, CA 94710

www.softskull.com
www.counterpointpress.com

Distributed by Publishers Group West

10 9 8 7 6 5 4 3 2 1

Many thanks to the editors of the following magazines where some of these pages first appeared: *Bern Porter International, canwehaveourballback, Chiron Review, Columbia Poetry Review, Exquisite Corpse, Iris, ixnay, La Petite Zine, Oyster Boy Review, Painted Bride Quarterly, Pearl, Powhatan Review, RFD, River City Review, The South 666 Bitch*, and *Still*.

Many thanks to the editors of the following anthologies where some of these pages first appeared: *Why Are Faggots So Afraid of Faggots*, edited by Mattilda Bernstein Sycamore. *Everything I Have Is Blue: Short Fiction by Working-Class Men about More-or-Less Gay Life*, edited by Wendell Ricketts.

Some of these pages were performed by the Blue Rose Theater Company's production of *Elvisito Loco* at the Philadelphia Fringe Festival.

Some of these pages were included in a collaborative project with Frank Sherlock titled *The B. Franklin Basement Tapes* for NEXUS Gallery's 300th birthday celebration of Benjamin Franklin in Philadelphia.

Thanks to Ken and Jonas for the Swahili lesson, and to everyone in Philadelphia who called the ELVIS line. Much Love and Respect to Greg Fuchs, Jonathan Allen, Buck Downs, and Charles Wolski. Thanks to Edwin Hermance for the Sappho "R" info. Big thanks to my amazing friends, but especially Frank Sherlock, Elizabeth Kirwin, Maria Raha, Heather Raquel Phillips, Ben Malkin, Matthue Roth, Magdalena Zurawski, Maria Mirabal, Dorothea Lasky, Thom Donovan, Mary Kalyna, Eileen Myles, Susie Timmons, Jenn & Chris McCreary, Nail & Prank, Cathleen Miller, Maria Fama, Ish Klein, Jen Hess, Hassen, and many others! A special thanks to Anne Horowitz and Adam Krefman at Soft Skull Press for all of their hard work! And to Goodloe Byron for the fantastic cover! Thanks too to our great diva Freya Aswynn for spiritual advice about the book. My heart belongs to the good people of Memphis and Philadelphia, two islands of Love!

one

"Do You Know the Way to San Jose"

is not an Elvis song

They used to say there were two shows at an Elvis concert: the one on stage, the other off stage in the audience. Well Elvis, guess it's strictly our show now, in your honor of course.

"The audience is the other half of me."

—Elvis

Twelve apostles and no rock band. Jesus had enough guys for an entire touring company: publicist, sound man, matzo baker, manager, and enough left over for a four piece band. Four Beatles was apparently enough. There's no doubt Jesus had the attitude to rock Rome. He lived long enough for six or seven gold records, and he could have eventually gone solo, a duet or two with Mary Magdalene. Oh well, Bethlehem is still probably a lot like Memphis, curio shops selling Jesus fountain pens and Jesus belt buckles, his favorite foods served at a nice desert café, Joseph's carpentry shop now complete with Black & Decker power tools. The main difference of course between Jesus H. Christ and Elvis Aaron Presley—besides sandals and Cadillacs—is Elvis had more fun liberating His people. By the way, what's the H for in Jesus's name?

I took a speeding taxi, not meaning to take a speeding taxi. "Elvis died in 1977, there's really no rush," I wanted to say, but didn't. The maniac driver turned the wheel with his body, screaming at other cars. I just let it happen, zooming along. Stopped at a traffic light, there were rabbits in someone's garden, stalking cabbage. Then zooming again, Memphis a blur. To counter his urgency I slowly unbent my fingers, then slowly bent my fingers, inches from my face, creak in the body, over, and slowly over again. My entire being fixed on the slowness I am capable of, bending, unbending. So. Slow. Then we lurched to a halt, he spun around, smiling, "Six dollars please thank you!"

Elvis and his parents are buried in Graceland's Meditation Garden.
I met Maisy from Mobile, Alabama, kneeling in prayer. She's a lot
of fun. I guess she's in her 50s, bright red hair, Elvis jewelry, Elvis
T-shirt. We had lunch near the Elvis Automobile Museum.

MAISY: (looking at my cafeteria tray) Conrad Darlin', all I see on
that tray is vegetables. Don't you want meatloaf? Elvis loved meatloaf. Priscilla once said He ate meatloaf everyday for six months.

ME: I'm a vegetarian.

MAISY: Vegetarian!? My stars, what kind of Elvis fan are you!?

ME: I'm on the Advanced Elvis Course.

MAISY: Advanced Elvis Course!? Oh, good one. So, ah, where's your
wife anyway?

ME: I'm gay.

MAISY: OOOOOOOOOOH! So, you like Elvis tooooooo. You're just
full of surprises. Well, that's all right, everyone thought I was a
lesbian in high school. I was just in love with Elvis and saving
myself for His lovin' touch, you know.

ME: Are you still a virgin?

MAISY: (screams) OH! My goodness no! You sure are nosey, I like
that. I'm not a virgin, but I'll tell you, the first time I got balled I

pretended he was Elvis. Mmm. Uh, well, he was too clumsy and selfish for the fantasy to really work though. The only other man I loved more than Elvis was Lester Parker. And he was gay, like you. Elvis is dead now, Lester is still gay, and my ex-husband Ricky works the casinos in Vegas.

ME: So you're divorced?

MAISY: YES thank God! Divorced six years this Halloween! Now I've got a vibrator named Elvis. And a dog named Hound Dog. Only, he ain't a hound dog, he's a poodle.

*T*here are drinking glasses in the locked cabinets of Graceland with Elvis' engraved initials: EAP. They sure are nice drinking glasses. EAP. Most 20th-century drinking glasses will have to wait hundreds of years before they make it into a museum. Lucky EAPs!

It was the summer snow of Memphis is what it was. I saw it from Graceland's front step. A light shower of snow falling to the ground beneath one large tree in the yard. "Did you see that?" I asked a nearby woman. "Yeah, what was it? It looked like snow." I walked quickly to the tree while the guards weren't looking (they're Nazis about you walking on the grass whether or not you've just seen the only August snow in America fall on Elvis' front yard). It was gone. But the air was cool, like there was an air conditioner inside that tree. I looked up into its vast spread of leaves. There was nothing unusual about it, except for the fact it just shook snow from its branches in 97 degrees of humid Tennessee air. What was it? Well, it was the summer snow of Memphis is what it was. "Hey you, get the hell off the grass!"

Maisy introduced me to her aunt Sandy who drove by tonight to pick her up.

MAISY: Sandy, come on out here'n meet Conrad.

ME: Hi Sandy.

SANDY: Nice to meet you there Conrad.

MAISY: Conrad's a vegetarian, and he's gay.

SANDY: Uh, all right, whatever Maisy honey, whatever.

MAISY: Conrad, we're about to head on over to Pirtle's Chicken. I know you don't eat meat.

SANDY: But they sure have good corn biscuits.

MAISY: Problem is the chicken though. Twenty-one ways to cook a chicken. And you're a vegetarian and all.

ME: More important than being a vegetarian though is I'm gay, and gay people don't eat chicken.

SANDY: Huh? What's he talkin' about Maisy?

MAISY: I don't know, I mean, I never knew too many gay people.

ME: Did Elvis eat chicken?

MAISY: Yes.

ME: Are you sure?

SANDY: Positive, yes!

Onboard the Lisa Marie jet for a tour of what Elvis called his "Graceland in the Sky," I couldn't help but think of my uncle who wanted to be a pilot for United Airlines. He always dreamt of flying one of those big jets from Cleveland to Hawaii everyday, ever since he saw Elvis in *Blue Hawaii*. My uncle wound up driving a bus for Greyhound after failing pilot school. I used to imagine him driving a bus load of passengers from Cleveland to San Diego, pulling over at the coast, gazing out over the Pacific, picturing Hawaii thousands of miles away, beaches full of airline pilots reclining with piña coladas and cheeseburgers. San Diego is about as close to Hawaii a Greyhound bus could ever hope to get. My uncle died a sick, bitter man, having to drive from Cleveland to San Diego every week, the bus never lifting off the ground, no pretty stewardesses pacing up and down aisles handing out peanuts and pillows. He would have loved the Lisa Marie jet. "Wow, this sure is classy," he'd have said, sitting down in the pilot's seat. "You know, those airline pilots all think they're such hot shit! I could've flown one of these things, no problem! Those fucking pilots are nothing more than glorified bus drivers if you ask me! Who the fuck do they think they're kidding!? Sons of bitches!"

In the Meditation Garden this afternoon an old woman with a portable oxygen tank knelt at the foot of Elvis' grave. She then stood in front of the graves of his parents Gladys and Vernon.

WOMAN: You raised a decent boy. I'm glad I got here one more time, like I promised. I'll be seeing you all soon.

She handed her husband a small silver bottle on a thin chain. He plucked some grass from Elvis' grave, sealed it in the bottle, then placed it around her neck. A little girl approached.

GIRL: (pointing to the silver bottle) What's that for?

WOMAN: (smiling) I'm going to take it to heaven with me. The King misses his home. I made him a promise in a dream.

"Could I get mail sent to Graceland for me, just once? It would mean so much to me."

"No!"

"Please?"

"Who is going to send you mail to Graceland!?"

"I'll ask someone to write me a letter, or ask Disney World to send me another catalog."

"No!"

"Please, it would mean so much to me."

"No!"

• INSTRUCTIONS •
FOR ELVIS-GUIDED TOURS OF MEMPHIS

There's no better way to see Memphis than asking the man who loved Memphis best! Put your favorite Elvis in an iPod or CD player, start from any point in Memphis, and walk. Get going. Trust Elvis.

Feel Him. You'll know what I mean when you feel Him. Let your steps flow with the words to His song:

> *Step into my heart.*
> *Leave your cares behind.*
> *Welcome to my world,*
> *built with you in mind.*

My friend Ken and I could never feel Elvis the same. We'd be driving down the road listening to "It's Now Or Never." As soon as Elvis reached His peak in the song, Ken would turn the volume down a notch.

ME: Ken, you're doing it again.

KEN: What?

ME: Every time Elvis hits His peak you turn Him down, you dampen His flame.

KEN: I don't know, it just gets too loud.

ME: Ken, the volume is consistent throughout the song. You compensate volume for the vibration Elvis puts in you.

KEN: What the fuck are you talking about!?

ME: I'm trying to tell you you're afraid of the vibration of Elvis.

KEN: That's bullshit!

ME: No it's not.

KEN: Yes it is!

ME: No it's not.

KEN: Yes it is! Now shut the fuck up!

ME: All right. Have it your way.

KEN: Good! I will have it my way!

ME: There's no shame in being afraid of Elvis though.

KEN: I'm not afraid! If you don't shut your mouth I'm gonna pull over and kick the shit out of you!

• 2 HOLY CITIES OF AMERICA •

Democracy (another kind of rock 'n' roll) began in Philadelphia. Rock 'n' roll (another kind of democracy) began in Memphis. Benjamin Franklin and Elvis Presley, two great leaders in the rhythm of freedom, never met, due to the technicality that Benjamin Franklin died 145 years before the birth of Elvis Presley. This should not however prevent us from delighting in the assumption that if Benjamin Franklin had survived, the two would have become fast and loyal friends. Benjamin Franklin would have no doubt been a regular at Graceland for suppers, bouncing little Lisa Marie on his two-hundred-year-old knee, telling gossip about George Washington and that insufferable prick John Adams. Elvis would have taught the old man a few dance steps to drive the women crazy, then taken him out to the firing range to shoot targets of King George and his British Red Coats for old times' sake. Oh those would have been great times, would have made some great American portraits, two American fathers of Liberation.

There's no such thing as coming to Graceland by yourself. You'll be eating fried peanut butter banana sandwiches with new friends in no time, playing the All-Elvis Wurlitzer jukebox.

ME: What song you playing next Maisy?

MAISY: Hell I don't know, it's all Elvis, so you can't go wrong. Right? I just put my money in and push the buttons. Let Him surprise me. I like it when Elvis surprises me.

It's sad to report there's no one left in Philadelphia who remembers meeting Benjamin Franklin. We were all born too late in American history. Damn! But there's nothing we can do about it. At the beginning of the 21st century there's still plenty of folks around Memphis who knew Elvis Presley though. Isn't that exciting!? The problem is how to meet them. Place an advertisement? Carry a sign? I decided to listen to Elvis' music on my portable CD player and let Him guide me through Memphis, let Him lead me to His people. Today for instance, I was listening to "Kentucky Rain" on Jefferson Street in downtown Memphis:

> *showed your photograph*
> *to some old gray-bearded men*
> *sitting on a bench outside*
> *a general store*
> *they said "Yes she's been here"*
> *but their memory wasn't clear*

All of a sudden an old man came around the corner. "Elvis!? You knew this old man didn't you!?"

ME: (excited) Excuse me sir!?

OLD MAN: Eh? What?

ME: Did you know Elvis Presley?

OLD MAN: Elvis Presley!? No! What on earth makes you think that!?

"The ones that work days in cities and the ones that work nights in cities, they live in different cities. The cities have the same name but they are different cities. As different as night and day. There's something wild in the country that only the night people know."

—Tennessee Williams, from *Orpheus Descending*

Saturday nights on Beale Street are just amazing! A different live blues singer pouring from every open door you pass. At one busy intersection preachers climb onto milk crates, waving bibles in the neon glow, shouting about Jesus and hell and sin and, you know their story. What I love is the energy of the hecklers.

> Fuck off!
> Yeah! Fuck off!
> Lighten up preacher boys!
> —God! . . . Hell! . . . Jesus! . . .
> Christ dead! . . . Only son! . . .
> Ah, fuck off!
> Cold beer! Git yer cold beer!

I overheard a young woman say to her boyfriend, "Now why is it they think we can't get loose, have a good time, and still believe in the power of the Lord?"

I said loud enough for her to hear, "The power of Elvis!"

She turned to me with an excited glint in her eye, "Yeah! The power of Elvis!" Her boyfriend glared at me. She shouted at the preachers, "The power of Elvis! The power of Elvis! Woooooooooooeeeeeeeeee!"

Someone else shouted, "Yeah! Elvis man! Elvis! Elvis! Elvis! Elvis!"

I smiled and said hello to her glaring boyfriend to put him at ease. He nodded and acted like they were a sailboat catching a wind moving quickly and far away from me.

I had sex with a hot nerd I met on Beale Street in a blues bar. A beautiful brown-eyed computer geek with smoldering sideburns and a huge cock, MMMMM, M is for Memphis Trophy!

That night I dreamt Elvis was naked, asleep on his back. I thought, "WOW, His cock looks exactly like that hot nerd's cock!" Semen leaked onto His thigh, large white tadpoles that crawled across the bed, up the wall, and over my head. They had little angry faces and sharp teeth, and dropped into my open mouth, attacking my tongue, the sperm and blood a delicious combination!

I woke to find my hot nerd smiling at me, waiting to clobber me with his stiffy! I told him my dream, which turned him on. "Let me be your Elvis this morning," he whispered.

In Philadelphia, every Sunday morning between 7:00 AM and 10:00 AM is the Elvis show on radio station WOGL. This is one Sunday service that won't put you to sleep, filled with bits of interviews and music proclaiming His message of love and brotherhood, as only Elvis Himself could tell it.

Maisy and I are eating fried peanut butter banana sandwiches.

MAISY: Conrad honey, is this sandwich part of the Advanced Elvis Course?

ME: Well, it's not ideal, but at least there's no meat.

MAISY: No dead moo cow on our fried peanut butter banana sandwich? Praise Jesus!

ME: Praise Elvis!

MAISY: Oh, I guess that's what I meant. I get them two mixed up all the time.

ME: You said your vibrator's name is Elvis.

MAISY: Oh Conrad! I never mix them up when I'm doin' that! You can be sure!

In the Elvis Automobile Museum
in the men's room
in the urinal
there's a rubber splash mat that says exactly:

Say
No
to Drugs

Swisher

1-800-444-4138

I didn't flush.

*O*ne of the most fascinating human beings visited Graceland today. She wore a floor-length brown robe held together by a beige, tattered rope that could have been cut from a 16th-century bell tower. Her hair was gray with tints of mousey red. Her eye glass frames were clear plastic with tiny, thin flecks of black that looked like beetle legs. The lenses were pale yellow and thick, giving her oversized, yellow eyes. She wore a giant blood-red insignia ring of some ancient order of dragon slayers on her hand and a large crucifix around her neck I swear looked as if it were made from compressed laundry soap flakes. Her skin was very white, like she was clear plastic filled with Vitamin D Whole Milk. All this and bright white Adidas tennis shoes with zero scuff marks, her guardian angel constantly buffed and wiped them all day long, unseen. She had a giant, almost frightening smile that nobody seemed able to interpret comfortably. Was it friendly? Was it hungry and cannibalistic? Was it holy, or on the absolute edge of sanity? She was endlessly fascinating and completely alone, though she pointed to display cases of gold records and nodded, as though she and her invisible friends had just been discussing the very items displayed. Her glowing moment however came in the meditation garden. She was standing in front of Gladys Presley's grave. She held her arms as though she held warm invisible towels for the pope. She didn't make a sound, yet moved her mouth as though she addressed a crowd of thousands, throwing her head around, opening her mouth as far as it would go, all this, with, no, sound. After a bit of this she put her arms down and glided away. I never saw her again, though I kept an eye out for her the rest of the day. It's as though she slipped through some slit in the air between Graceland and the parking lot. Poof! I missed her almost instantly, the way someone misses a favorite television program that has been taken off the air forever and there is no channel in all the world interested in ever showing reruns.

• WHO COMES TO GRACELAND? •
Inventory of parking lot:

3 limousines.

8 RVs.

9 mini vans.

18 Harley-Davidson motorcycles parked together.

22 station wagons.

4 Volkswagen Bugs.

6 rusted Pintos
(One reads "GRACELAND OR BUST!" on back windshield).

15 chartered buses.

12 Corvettes.

1 beat up black hearse with a smiley face sticker
on its rusted bumper.

50 to 60 various Fords and other normal cars.

8 Cadillacs (1 pink).

1 very odd vehicle that is a cross between an Army Jeep
and Marilyn Monroe's little vixen under panties,
like *Viva Las Vegas* meets *G.I. Blues*.

$\mathcal{M}$ike from Seattle and I discovered we both write poetry when we got to talking.

MIKE: Poets have a hard time accepting the death of their youth.

ME: As opposed to everyone else?

MIKE: Yeah! I mean, look at Frank Stanford, look at Plath.

ME: Now how would Elvis feel about that, Mike?

MIKE: Elvis!? What's Elvis got to do with it!?

ME: We're sitting in the Graceland parking lot eating fried peanut butter banana sandwiches, Elvis has everything to do with it.

MIKE: Oh. Well, do you consider yourself a poet or not?

ME: Yes! There's a poet in all of us!

In the Graceland kitchen you can look right into the cabinet full of dinnerware. There's a beautiful matching set with little painted cherries or cranberries, I'm not sure which—cherries and cranberries always look the same to me. Now, if you look in the left side of the cabinet you'll see a bowl with little painted cherries or cranberries with a chip out of the side of it. Graceland has a bowl with a chip out of the side of it! Why didn't Elvis do something about it!?

(The Presleys at the supper table.)

ELVIS: Priscilla, can you believe this damn bowl has a chip out of the side of it?

PRISCILLA: Oh. Well, it's still a beautiful bowl.

ELVIS: All right honey, you're right, you're right.

(Or maybe.)

ELVIS: Priscilla, can you believe this damn bowl has a chip out of the side of it?

PRISCILLA: Don't you remember Darlin', Keith Richards did that when he and Mick were here for supper?

ELVIS: Oh yeah, yeah, that's right. Well, guess we should save it then.

(Or maybe.)

ELVIS: Priscilla, can you believe this damn bowl has a chip out of the side of it?

PRISCILLA: Where? I don't see anything.

ELVIS: (blink, blink) Oh, okay. I swore I saw a chip out of the side of that bowl. Say Priscilla Sugar, are these damn things cherries or cranberries painted on our dinnerware?

The onion sandwich
on a bed of parsley
and flower petals.
Priscilla spins

and whirls in her wedding gown as the band plays and the families cheer her on. Poor little onion sandwich, all alone, piles of pastrami and olives nearby. The cook only had time to make one onion sandwich. To be an onion sandwich at such an event, all alone. Oh. Everyone loves an onion sandwich, but there's only one. Aunts, uncles, everyone wants to be polite at such an event, no one wants to eat the only onion sandwich. Elvis stands nearby, smiling, glass of champagne in hand, imagining the hotel room that awaits him and his gorgeous bride. Priscilla could eat the onion sandwich—it's her day after all. Her aunts, although each of them wants the onion sandwich for themselves, they will do their best to convince her she should have the onion sandwich. It's her special day after all. But she was raised properly, and she'll politely decline, since it's the only onion sandwich around.

There are always 108 steps between you and Elvis wherever you are

(notice there was no mention of the size of the steps)

Overheard this conversation in Shoney's Restaurant from a table of two women and one man.

MAN: Although Elvis is undoubtedly Hermes. But, yet, He's remarkably got the stamp of the African god Shango.

WOMAN: ALL RIGHT ALREADY! Shut up! Elvis is Elvis and that's that! He's not like anybody! END of story! Now, I'm telling you, I don't want to hear anymore of this nonsense you never shut up about! (to the other woman) Honestly, you just don't have any idea what it's been like! I've been hearing this for days now! First on the plane, then on the bus, then in the taxi, then in the bar at the hotel where I had to get myself a drink just to be able to put up with it all! Enough's enough already! Let me eat my fucking cheeseburger in peace! Elvis is Elvis! He's not like anybody!

When the ancient rulers of Memphis, Egypt were put to rest, drawings of a handsome man in blue shoes covered the pyramid walls. The hieroglyphs, once deciphered, appeared to be the lost, original lyrics to "Love Me Tender."

Understand it is He who adds to what you thought complete.

I wanted an Elvis T-shirt. There are at least ten shops in Memphis that sell Elvis souvenirs—you'd think it wouldn't be a problem. There are literally dozens of different Elvis T-shirts to choose from. Then I found it. It was blue, the blue of Krishna's beautiful skin.

> "God is a living presence in all of us."
> —Elvis

The truth of the matter is if Elvis and Priscilla ever had a yard sale on the long lawns of Graceland they would have sold everything in three minutes, customers screaming, crushing one another to buy the King's used socket wrenches and ashtrays. It used to take me hours to sell only half the things my mother wanted to get rid of. We had a set of Sonny & Cher napkin rings that always wound up back in the attic 'til next summer's yard sale. For five years I put on my finest Capricorn salesmanship, "And over here, ma'am, we have a lovely set of Sonny & Cher napkin rings." None of our yard sale customers ever had dinner events fancy enough to employ the likes of Sonny & Cher napkin rings. Of course neither did we, that's why we wanted someone else to get stuck never using them. A set of Sonny & Cher napkin rings at Elvis' yard sale would have been swiped up by some shrieking, weeping yard-sale customer. If Elvis had dropped by my own yard sale and just touched my Sonny & Cher napkin rings they would have been transformed into the Sonny & Cher Touched By Elvis Napkin Rings. Every one of my shrieking, weeping yard-sale customers (it was very uncommon for me to ever have shrieking, weeping yard-sale customers) would have wanted one of the eight Sonny & Cher Touched By Elvis Napkin Rings. No one would have had a complete set! Yeah, Elvis would have been a big help back then. But He had His own successful three-minute yard sale to worry about. Only a few other Americans could have had yard sales as successful as Elvis'—the president for instance as long as he was still in office; no one wants to buy used rollerskates from an ex-president. I wonder if Jackie O was ever given a complimentary set of Sonny & Cher napkin rings? When she smiled for a photograph with them in her hands they would have become the Sonny & Cher Touched By Jackie O While Being Photographed Napkin Rings. Is it true there were also Elvis & Priscilla napkin rings? Did Sonny & Cher have a set?

"The President lives in Washington, D.C.,
but the King is from Memphis!"
—graffiti on the Graceland Wall

In the second grade Mrs. Eedshid had a ceramic Elvis-head planter. He sat on the edge of her desk looking over our alphabet eyes with His short, fresh clip of ivy haircut, which, by the end of the year was a full-globe afro. My mother and her new boyfriend were always getting stoned and tormenting my seriousness for the second grade.

MOM: Hey, what's that teacher's name?

ME: Mrs. Eedshid.
(they crack up laughing)

MOM: Ah man! Mrs. Eat Shit! What a name man!

ME: NO! It's Mrs. Eeeeeeedshid! Eeeeedshid! *She's very very nice!*
(they crack up laughing again)

My seriousness and repeated, highly emphasized correction of their pronunciation of Mrs. Eedshid's name always remained a source of endless entertainment, usually leaving them rolling into one another with uncontrollable laughter.

Sometime during the third grade it seemed appropriate to pay a visit to my old second-grade classroom to show them what it looked like to be a sophisticated third grader. Second grade was far behind me now, but I was willing to make an appearance, maybe give a little guest speech or take questions if necessary. Mrs. Eedshid had been replaced by a thin-faced, scary-looking man. Class had not started, everyone was talking and pulling out their homework. The Elvis-head planter was still at the edge of the desk, ivy hair by this time spilling over the sides, almost to the floor. With His beautiful, unanticipated long hair, Elvis resembled a good man I was beginning to hear about. A man who used to live in the desert with twelve other good men. A man of magic and power who had come to rescue us all from the narrow, rigid world. Like the world before rock 'n' roll.

11:00 AM every morning at the Peabody Hotel in Memphis is the duck walk. A man brings them down from the penthouse elevator and walks them out to the fountain for a swim.

WOMAN: (to her little daughter) Look at the ducks honey, look. (to an old woman) So this is a Memphis tradition?

OLD WOMAN: Oh yes, yes indeed.

WOMAN: We're here to visit Graceland. Do you think Elvis ever saw this duck walk tradition?

OLD WOMAN: Oh my yes. I saw Him down here once many years back with His little daughter Lisa Marie. That was many years ago, she couldn't have been more than two or three, like your little girl. I remember He seemed so happy pointing to the ducks. People said He had problems, drugs and alcohol, but I think He was a good father. He really loved little Lisa Marie.

*W*hile catching a breath between "Jailhouse Rock" and "Don't Be Cruel" in His famous 1968 Comeback Concert, Elvis picks up the mic stand like a harpoon and shouts "MOBY DICK!"

Why would Elvis reference Melville between "Jailhouse Rock" and "Don't Be Cruel"????? I'm sitting on the bank of the Mississippi, Arkansas is on the other side. I'm staring at the colors of the setting sun on the passing river like I'm running out of time, like I need to find the cure, "Moby Dick? MobyDickMobyDickMobyDick. Hm." You can stare at the passing Mississippi all you want but Melville won't come any clearer.

"Consider, once more, the universal cannibalism of the sea;
all whose creatures prey upon each other, carrying
on eternal war since the world began."
—Herman Melville, from *Moby Dick*

The Memphis visitor's center is open twenty-four hours on the bank of the Mississippi. They have a movie screen continuously showing Elvis' 1968 comeback concert. I watched it three times tonight.

Three very drunk women from Tampa came in, one of them screamed, "Holy shit! It's the king on the big screen!" Elvis was singing "All Shook Up" for the third time tonight. They dropped their bags and started dancing and whooping, "Whoop! Whoop! All shook up! Yeah! Yeah!" One of them spotted me "C'mon baby! Dance with me baby!" After a couple of dance tunes came "Love Me Tender." We stood there swaying together, staring at the black leather of Elvis fold and unfurl in the 1968 stage lights. The end of the song is perfect, he thrusts both arms in the air, head hanging low, it's really quite glorious! We were well connected (like all good Elvis fans) and fell to our knees together, touching our heads to the ground, the ancient head-below-the-heart sign of reverence. One woman spoke for us all, "Oh Elvis, Elvis, we love and worship you!" There were four of us, the number of balance. Air, Fire, Water, Earth. Spring, Summer, Fall, Winter. Elvis was the fifth and larger element that shifts and delights the four.

Gloria, Virginia, and Dorothy were their names. I told them about the early morning meditation at Graceland. We went back to their hotel. There was only one bed—they had snuck into a room for one—so it would be cheaper.

ME: Doesn't the manager keep watch?

GLORIA: Are you kidding? Man I wanted ice for my ice bucket last night and had to practically blow the place up to get his attention away from the damn TV.

ME: Where are we going to sleep?

GLORIA: Well now I was hoping you'd get around to asking that.

VIRGINIA: You can sleep with me.

GLORIA: Or me.

DOROTHY: I don't care where he sleeps.

GLORIA: (rolls her eyes) She's a lesbian.

ME: So am I! I mean, I'm gay.

DOROTHY: No shit? Hey, cool brother. All right man, give me five!

VIRGINIA: Not again!

GLORIA: Man! I want to get laid in Memphis! I heard it's the easiest town to get laid in! Shit! I don't understand, I mean, I know I'm not Priscilla Presley, but I'm not ugly.

DOROTHY: I think you're hot Gloria.

GLORIA: Thanks but no thanks Dorothy honey.

VIRGINIA: Dotty's right sweetie, you're hot! You've had lots more boyfriends than me. You told me once you had so many boy-friends you don't remember how many. And I remember how many I've had.

GLORIA: Thanks Virginia honey, I'm just feeling sorry for myself is all. Thanks sweetie.

his morning we stand outside the gates to Graceland singing "How Great Thou Art." Elvis brings us together from France, China, England, Israel, Mexico, and yes, Philadelphia. Finally the guard comes to let us in, shaking his head. I turn to a woman, "You know, when we sing 'How Great Thou Art' we're singing to Elvis, not Jesus." She smiles, "Oh, you know it brother!"

Elvis is not a man. He ceased being a man in the 1950s as His songs and movies gathered the consciousness of millions. Can prayers to Elvis cure the sick and strengthen the weak? Absolutely, without a doubt. The collective focus of millions of people does not invoke but create a power out of naming it, believing in the name. Laugh at this and you are indeed a fool. Elvis is another opportunity for spiritual beings to raise our tower of energy and love we know we possess. Say His name, hold onto your dream, and be healed in the channel with us.

In the Hot Rod diner I met Fern and Burle from Louisiana.

FERN: Is your accent northern?

ME: Philadelphia.

FERN: (excited) My cousin Angela Thompson lives in Philadelphia! Do you know her!?

ME: Sorry, I don't.

FERN: Oh.

BURLE: Philadelphia's a big place.

ME: So, do you feel Elvis is still here?

FERN: Well yes, of course He is! Let me tell you. (Her voice gets low and she leans into the table.) My friend Charlotte was up here to Graceland a couple Christmases back. She took a picture in the house. Now, you're not suppose to use flash, but she said no one was looking. If you saw this photograph you'd never ask again.

BURLE: That's right.

FERN: Burle knows what I'm talkin' about.

BURLE: Mm hm.

ME: (I knew I was suppose to ask "What did you see in the photo-graph?") What did you see in the photograph?

FERN: (whisper) Elvis! (regular voice) Only, He's white light. Fuzzy, but it's him!

BURLE: That's right.

FERN: There's this crest of light up here on top, that's His hair. His hair was very important to His image and message you know.

ME: The power of Elvis!

FERN: (pointing at me) You got it! The power of Elvis! Well it's Him all right. And they know He's here too, that's why we aren't sup-posed to go upstairs, in the bathroom where He died, or His bed-room, over half the house!

ME: What room did she take the photograph in?

BURLE: The pool room.

FERN: That's right! Standing next to the pool table under that ceil-ing of pleated fabric. It's just amazing!

BURLE: Yes it is.

• IF ELVIS IS NOT PARANOID •
SOMEONE WILL HAVE TO DO IT FOR HIM

Elvis can't hide the fact He has a penis. He's walking down the street and everyone knows He has a penis! It's outrageous! How dare they! But there's virtually nothing He can do about it. And they imagine other penises they've seen to imagine His penis. Which isn't fair either, but He's not whipping it out to say, "Hey, stop imagining things, this is mine! This is mine!" He's sick of it! Sick sick sick sick of it! How dare they think about His penis! But there's nothing He can do about it. The best thing to do is not mention it. When someone walks up to Him and begins a conversation about the expected rainfall this afternoon He just keeps talking about rain, never saying, "I know you know I have a penis!" It's ridiculous He should even have to say such a thing! But it's the way the world is! Better to ignore. Yes, ignore. That's it, that's best.

I met a woman named Myra. She was flipping rapidly through the Graceland guide book. I asked her for the time.

MYRA: (very New York accent) Oh yeah, 2:30.

ME: Thank you.

MYRA: My God! 2:30! I only have two hours before I have to be back at the airport!

ME: Two hours!? I've been here for days and haven't seen it all.

MYRA: Listen, I'm from New York! I could do Memphis in an hour!

ME: I'm from Philadelphia.

MYRA: Oh. My cousin Sidney lives in Philadelphia.

ME: Oh, I don't know him.

MYRA: What? Well of course you don't, Philadelphia's a big place!

I wish I liked coffee. The array of Elvis coffee mugs in the gift shop are wonderful on the eyes. But I don't like coffee. I wish I liked coffee . . . but I don't. Why not apple juice, or soda in a beautiful Elvis coffee mug? Well, I don't know. It just doesn't seem right. Something maybe my mother said when I was young, "What's the matter with you!? That's a coffee mug! They're for coffee, not milk!" I don't know for sure, it's lost to me. Oh well. A very polite southern woman with a gift shop name tag approaches me, "May I help you sir?" "Oh, no thanks." But those sure are nice Elvis coffee mugs. I wish coffee was delicious to me. I wish every morning I was excited by the smell of coffee! But I'm not, in fact I hate coffee. I could buy a beautiful Elvis coffee mug just in case I one day discover the wonders of coffee drinking, but I know I won't. It's not ever going to happen.

One more tour of Graceland.

MAISY: Oh my Lord! I get so horny every time I step a foot inside this house!

GLORIA: Oh Sugar, I know exactly what you mean. How about you Conrad, you horny? (she grabs my cock through my pants) Nope, Conrad's not. C'mon Conrad, don't you just want to take some guy up to Elvis' bed and do him!? Goddamn, you came a long way, it's the least they can let you do if you ask me.

ME: Sure, sex in Elvis' bedroom would be worth dying for.

MAISY: I'd like to have sex in the kitchen. What a kitchen!

GLORIA: Sounds good to me Maisy honey, have someone fry me up a hamburger for a little post-romance snack. What d'ya say Conrad, hm? A burger after you get the buns?

MAISY: He's a vegetarian.

GLORIA: What!? Wait a minute! Conrad, now, let me get this straight, so to speak. You don't fuck women, and you don't eat meat? What kind of Elvis fan are you? Please tell me you at least do drugs!? Christ!

ME: I'm on the Advanced Elvis Course.

GLORIA: The what? What the fuck is that!?

VIRGINIA: I want to have sex in Elvis' jet!

MAISY: The one He named after His daughter?

GLORIA: By the way, speaking of Lisa Marie, where is that girl? Where's her manners? She should be down here making us coffee.

ME: And throwing us the keys to her daddy's bedroom.

GLORIA: Now you're talkin' Conrad! Damn boy! I'm gonna take you to Beale Street tonight and buy you a beer! You do drink beer don't you? Conrad, you're gonna drink a beer tonight if I have to shove a funnel in your face and pour it down ya!

VIRGINIA: Oh My God, look at that photograph of Priscilla on the wall!

GLORIA: Wow, she was so gorgeous! Hey, where the hell's Dorothy? Dorothy honey, come look at whose portrait is hanging in Elvis' dining room!

VIRGINIA: Dorothy has the hots for Priscilla.

MAISY: Well I can see why. I'm not a lesbian and I have the hots for her.

ME: I know a couple of straight guys who have the hots for Elvis.

GLORIA: Yeah well, maybe it is true what those preachers said how the Presleys destroyed American values.

MAISY: Amen to that!

ME: And another amen!

VIRGINIA: And another amen!

MAISY: Boy, those security guards all look so mean. They're really watching us good.

GLORIA: Yeah well, they probably think we're gonna snag one of the King's ashtrays.

ME: They're treating us like we're white trash.

GLORIA: Conrad honey, I hate to burst your bubble but we are white trash. Don't you go fooling yourself, Advanced Elvis Course or not.

• MORE THAN ANYTHING •

more than anything, anything at all
I want permission from Lisa Marie to
spend one night in His bedroom,
on the floor, next to His bed,
naked, dressed in a body condom,
imagining I'm His happy little sperm,
after He's gone to sleep,
pressed to my condom wall,
looking to the moonlit window,
quietly, peacefully turning from a
thick, white, almond flavored cream
to a clear, sticky puddle,
the expired egg seeker,
once blissfully shot from
His hardened, kingly shaft,
oh man what a ride!

• ELVIS' BACKYARD •

something tickled the insides of trees
they started to shake and without
mouths did not laugh

> "THE REASON:
> Those who aren't Elvis
> Fans will never
> understand the Reason
> to be here. We, who love Him
> can't explain it."
> —graffiti on the Graceland wall

Gloria and I are eating fried peanut butter banana sandwiches in the shadow of the Lisa Marie jet.

GLORIA: So what is this Advanced Elvis Course anyway?

ME: Well, many of us who rally around Elvis were together in a previous life.

GLORIA: Oh yeah? How was that?

ME: Elvis ruled an ancient culture still undiscovered by *National Geographic.* Our tribal ceremonial magic, healing, even community politics, was based on connecting all six senses on a cellular level with drumming and dancing. A whole lot of percussion and movement, surrendering spirit. This was the original rock 'n' roll. But of course, like all fun happy people, we were conquered by the christians. Elvis promised to return one day and lead us home. His greatest trick was coming back as a christian Himself, with a warm, gentle Judas kiss from within. This time His culture of rock 'n' roll would conquer the world! Very few ever sang both rock 'n' roll and gospel with such matched intensity. His message says love of God and brotherhood are the same. And love, of any kind, can never be wrong.

GLORIA: You know, Elvis once said, "If you hate another human being you're hating part of yourself."

ME: Sounds good to me.

GLORIA: Yeah. So I always figure it's gotta be the same if you love another human being you're loving part of yourself.

• ELVIS AND THE ILLUSION •
OF HEMISPHERE

There are two windows on the wall. One for each of us. We fly through them and meet in the room. I come early, the sun catching me on its orange descent, reflecting off my back as I land on the floor, land in a rolling ball, a wreck as always. He never lands so clumsily. With Him it's easy, gliding perfectly on the leather heels of His shoes. I come early so He doesn't see me crashing against the setting sun. I love Him. I don't want Him to see me sprawled and confused. I love Him. My tender spots, my bruises, each of them a curiosity to Him as we fold and unfold on the long sheets. What time is it? I'm waiting. Last time, He didn't come at all. He does that sometimes. Once, I waited half the night, making tiny pictures of Him, a hundred pictures of Him, smiling. They glued together nicely into the shape of an animal, or man, whatever you want it to be. He still hadn't come when I woke in the night and I found myself flying out the window confused as I had never been about feelings. Then I was sure of my feelings the next time I saw Him. What is that? Where have I dropped something I couldn't find again without Him? He knows what time it is. He knows I know. If He were here I'd say I understand my feelings. Any minute now He will glide through the window, the scroll of white drapes blowing aside. I know he'll come. I know it, I know he will.

There are gay men I know who are only attracted to the fat Elvis, and you feel the soft purr as they talk about His chubby neck and breasts.

Some people get angry when debating how long Elvis was fat, furiously whittling it down to six months as though the dead are anything but thin.

Let me assure you that a photograph of the fat Elvis will not evaporate from your wall in six months. Yes, you can jerk off to it for the rest of your life, I promise.

Gloria and I had a farewell souvenir splurge. I applied for the Elvis Presley VISA charge card, which they will never ever give me, but for applying I received a free refrigerator magnet of Elvis crooning above the VISA trademark. Gloria bought an Elvis lollipop and promptly licked the crotch bare, then kept licking till He was curved, like He'd been kicked instead of licked down there.

GLORIA: Well Conrad, it's been nice meeting you.

ME: Yeah, it's been great meeting you too. I'm sure gonna miss Memphis. I already miss Graceland. I'd like to think of it as a second home. But, it's back to Philadelphia I go.

GLORIA: Hell, why don't you just move here?

ME: Are you kidding? I can't live somewhere Benjamin Franklin never lived.

GLORIA: I know exactly what you mean! I feel the same way about Bern's Steak House, that's why it's back to Tampa for me, baby!

"Men & Melons are hard to know."
—Benjamin Franklin

Waiting for the bus outside Graceland to take me downtown, a crow reminded me of my father as he landed in the street to eat a very flattened black and white kitten. I was five years old, sitting on the front step. My father ran a claw through his thick black hair and gathered my black and white kitten from the side of the road into a bag, still meowing, but barely alive. My mother's Patsy Cline record cried "Sweet dreams of you" behind me. My father started the car, then put the meowing bag to the exhaust pipe. Suddenly the record changed to Elvis singing "Are You Lonesome Tonight?" The meowing bag quieted with a breath of poison. "That's done," he said. My bus arrived, sending my father flapping to the top of a light pole. I would be downtown soon, many years away.

• POSSIBLE GRACELAND TWILIGHT •
IN AUGUST 1975

Elvis was home alone, a rare event. He decided to order a pizza delivery. He had never ordered a pizza delivery before—it would be fun. He sat on the front step waiting for the delivery boy to arrive in some beat-up, smoking old car. It would feel good to hand the kid a hundred dollar bill and tell him to keep the change. Money's a beautiful thing when it's spread around. Damn that's a beautiful sky. Cicadas singing, peaceful Tennessee summer night. Elvis waited more than an hour and realized someone at the pizza shop must have decided it was a prank phone call. "Delivery for what address? Are you kidding me man!? That's Graceland. Elvis doesn't eat pizza, it's some kids messing around!"

Dear X,

I'm sorry I haven't written since Memphis. There's a very wonderful, hard-to-explain shift inside me. What's going on with Elvis can only be described as the blossom of what was once, but lost, of all faith. The things I discovered, not only of myself, but of the recreation, the rethinking and transfiguration of the innerstellar. We are witness to a new god. And I am glad to be alive and sharing this birth before He too becomes drained of His original purpose. No group, not even the pagans with their boring old exhumed mumbling of chants can compare to the purity that is Elvis. People are gathered to share in the energy, healing, loving, pure, not greedy, not expecting anything from one another. None of us have rules, none of us have scripture, save the simple request of love in the songs Elvis sang. This morning I woke up and thought, "Maybe I've gone insane? Maybe this is what it is to have gone insane? How can I be sure?" But I haven't . . . really I haven't. I change nothing, don no special wardrobe, no fasting, no commanding, demanding, nothing like that. I don't even care if I'm the only person who believes in Elvis the way I do, though it's a comfort to have met hundreds who in fact do, people from Israel, people from Australia, from France, from Japan. . . . The beginning of all faith must be like this: Thought silly enough by outsiders to be ignored, and in that special place left to us, we weave the most healing magic, and understand in this beginning, how our collective force creates an egg of warmth, a cycle of radiation that can enter any one of us at any time with a simple focus on that egg, and bend the force, and only for the good, and love. I don't even believe Elvis guides us really. To me it's something we can bend and focus with the power many of us are coming to know we have. Elvis existed on this planet for reasons far beyond the dreams of Hollywood and record promotions. Our lives after His death have grown, not as a parasitic force on His grave, no not at all, in fact, my point is that Elvis, the man, is not even who is important, but what is important is the power of Elvis that we create, for it is we who create Him, and not the other way around.

"Elvis, you still give us 'nguvud
ya roho'—strength of heart.
Magic Elvis Club, Kenya"
—graffiti on the Graceland Wall

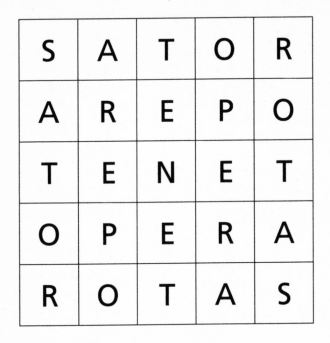

S	A	T	O	R
A	R	E	P	O
T	E	N	E	T
O	P	E	R	A
R	O	T	A	S

The Sator Formula
ancient magic square of protection

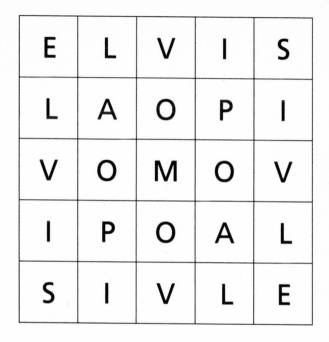

E	L	V	I	S
L	A	O	P	I
V	O	M	O	V
I	P	O	A	L
S	I	V	L	E

The Elvis Formula

new magic square of protection

The Elvis Mantra Chapter

HASSEN: "Did you say Elvis medicine chapter!?"

ME: Yes.

Ommmmmmm Elvis loves you
Elvis loves you Elvis loves yooooooou
Ommmmmmm Elvis loves you
Elvis loves you Elvis loves yooooooou

I open and close my hands
feel it in the air
open and close my hands

Ommmmmmm Elvis loves you
Elvis loves you Elvis loves yooooooou
Oh how much He loves yooooooou

The Philadelphia
Elvis Experiment

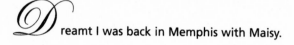reamt I was back in Memphis with Maisy.

MAISY: Every morning I touch my Elvis doll to my heart, to my head, to my heart again.

ME: Oh! Is that how we do devotions!?

MAISY: CONRAD! Elvis has no rules! It's whatever you do, it's your own special, personal devotion you make up on your own.

• 3 IMPERFECT DEVOTIONS •

press 45 of Love Me Tender
to stomach
then throat
then heart
then groin
then crown

dream of breast feeding
Elvis doll afraid of His white
choppers till pleasured by His
sucking then remember I'm not
a woman and it's blood He's
sucking but it's too late the
way you know it's too
late in dreams

hide photograph
of Elvis in my
underwear
giggling all
day on street
no one knows!
no one knows!
no one knows!

"The things that are most real to me are the illusions which I create with my painting. Everything else is a quicksand."

—Delacroix, 1824

The Delacroix exhibition came to the Philadelphia Museum of Art. I wore headphones, listening to my Elvis CD, letting Elvis guide me through the 19th-century paintings, letting Him feel our way from room to room. I wanted to spend time with the painting of Ovid in exile, but Elvis wanted lions, lions lions lions. He was singing "Don't Be Cruel," and I STOPPED in front of the painting titled *Young Woman Attacked By A Tiger.* "Don't be cruel, to a heart that's true . . ." What is it Elvis? What? What is it? "Baby it's just you I'm thinking of!"

In the gift shop there are Delacroix T-shirts, Delacroix postcards, Delacroix jigsaw puzzles, Delacroix baseball caps, Delacroix note pads, Delacroix video tapes, Delacroix pencils, and more! The yuppies rolled their eyes at my Elvis T-shirt and whispered to one another while purchasing their Delacroix coffee mugs. They're fools really. They think this gift shop is any different from Graceland with its Elvis wristwatches, Elvis cookie jars, and Elvis shot glasses. One man wearing a three-thousand-dollar Teton Brioni suit purchased a Delacroix baseball cap and CD titled *Music in the Time of Delacroix.* They're absurd Americans, just like me. We are the world's ridiculous, beautiful clowns. Get used to it my people!

"They are going to launch a large vessel called a clipper at noon today. Another of these American inventions to make people go faster and faster. When they have managed to get travellers comfortably seated inside a cannon so that they can be shot off like bullets in any given direction civilization will doubtless have taken a great step forward. We are making rapid strides towards that happy time when space will have been abolished; but they will never abolish boredom."

—From *The Journal of Eugene Delacroix*

I held Nail's hand in the tattoo shop while she had a purple heart tattooed over an ex-lover's name. Later she showed me her plastic appaloosa horse with parachute she threw into the air; we watched it slowly glide into the street.

NAIL: Hey man, mention my horse in your Elvis book.

ME: Why?

NAIL: I don't know.

ME: It's got nothing to do with Elvis.

NAIL: Um. Well. Hey I know dude! I'll name my horse Elvis! Yeah man!

ME: Elvis the Parachuting Plastic Appaloosa Horse?

NAIL: (throwing horse back into the air) Yeah man! Yeah! That's right! There it goes.

• THE NIGHT I WAS A LESBIAN SOUNDTRACK •

Hanging with my lesbian sisters Nail and Prank.

PRANK: Hey Conrad! Sing us that lesbian tune you made up.

ME: Bump-bump-bump-bump-beaver-bump-bump-bump-bump-beaver-beaver-bump-bump-bump-beaver-beaver-beaver-beaver-bump-beaver-bump-beaver-bump-bump-bump-bump-beaver-bump-bump-bump-bump-beaver-beaver-bump-bump-bump-bump.

NAIL: Whoa! That's so cool Conrad!

PRANK: Yeah dude!

ME: Thanks.

NAIL: It's like a lesbian anthem or something.

PRANK: A soundtrack! A fuck soundtrack!

NAIL: Yeah! A lesbian soundtrack! Cool!

PRANK: Hey Conrad! Man, put that on a tape recorder man!

ME: Okay.

NAIL: Yeah man, so we can bump our beavers to it man!

ME: Um, sure, okay.

PRANK: Dude, come sing it for us now man.

NAIL: Yeah man.

ME: What do you mean?

PRANK: (grabs my sleeve to lead me) In the bedroom, while Nail and I get it on.

ME: Huh? What!? Whoa!

NAIL: (takes my other sleeve) C'mon Connie man! It's almost Prank's birthday man!

ME: Prank's a Gemini! Your birthday's in June, Prank!

PRANK: C'mon Conrad. C'mon man.

ME: No way.

NAIL: (pulls my sleeve) C'mon dude!

PRANK: Yeah, it'll give you something fun to write about.

ME: I don't think so.

PRANK: C'mon, please? Please?

NAIL: Please? Conrad, c'mon Conrad, please?

ME: Oh my god!

NAIL: Please please please. All you gotta do is sit there 'n' sing your beaver song.

PRANK: You can face the other way man.

NAIL: Yeah, it'll be nice. It'll be so nice Connie, c'mon Connie.

ME: Oh . . . oh, all right I'll, um, if—

PRANK: (yanks my sleeve) Let's go dude!

ME: (following them) Oh my god what am I doing!

NAIL: Conrad, you don't believe in God.

PRANK: Yeah dude, you believe in Elvis, and He would definitely approve.

NAIL: Yeah, yeah He would. Prank's right about that.

Fingers of Elvis!
You wake thinking the Mother Elvis tit in your mouth!
Let us praise tit!
Fingers of Elvis!
Let us praise tit!
Fingers of Elvis!
Let us praise tit!

NAIL: Hey dude, Oscar Wilde once said, "I like Elvis Presley's music better than anybody's. It is so loud that one can talk the whole time without people hearing what one says." Did you know that?

ME: Nail? Um, Oscar Wilde died in 1900.

NAIL: I know, and he was really referring to Wagner, I just wanted to see how far away you are with this Elvis thing is all.

• THE ELVIS-WAS-BEN INTERVIEW •

If you need to find yourself a Benjamin Franklin scholar it's important to spend a little time in Philadelphia. They bubble to the surface like the burnt oats of a New World porridge. They're not as life-loving and friendly as Elvis scholars, but they have their moments. I interviewed one such burnt oat mulching across Philadelphia who, by the end of the interview, insisted his name never be mentioned. It seems such deeply controversial questions connecting Elvis and Franklin would send a shudder of disbelief throughout the academic circles of American History. The Benjamin Franklin scholar, who agreed to the tape recording of our interview, will be known hereafter as BFS.

ME: Is it true Benjamin Franklin is a distant relative of Elvis Presley?

BFS: Eh—did you say Elvis Presley? (smiles)

ME: Yes.

BFS: (laughs) No.

ME: How about the theory that Elvis Presley was the reincarnation of Benjamin Franklin?

BFS: What? Whose theory?

ME: Mine.

BFS: (frowning) Is this some kind of joke?

ME: No, not at all, in fact, didn't Ben—may I call him Ben?

BFS: I suppose so, it's not my name, no need to ask me for permission!

ME: Didn't Ben record a dream he had where he scrawled the mysterious word E-L-V-I-S? Wasn't he puzzled by this ELVIS word?

BFS: That's nonsense, no such thing ever happened!

ME: Did Ben have any strange eating habits? Like fried peanut butter banana sandwiches for instance?

BFS: I'm not going to answer that!

ME: Because it might be true?

BFS: Because your question is absurd!

ME: Isn't it true that Franklin had a very serious addiction to prescription drugs?

BFS: They didn't have Thrift Drugstores in 18th-century America!

ME: Maybe when he was in France?

BFS: All right! I've heard enough!

ME: Excuse me, sir, but is it true there is a conspiracy to withhold information connecting Benjamin Franklin to Elvis Presley!?

BFS: Young man, whatever you wish. I insist you withhold my name from this project of yours though! I want nothing to do with your, your Elvis thing!

Some people have no respect for Elvis.
They need to write a letter,
Elvis is standing next to them,
they scribble on the back of His beautiful
sacred hand just to see
if there's ink in the pen.
How dare they!

The book *A Changing World* **is always with him on the dirtiest** streets of Philadelphia. It looks like a textbook, photo of sheep and bright hills of grass on the cover. Sometimes he'll be sitting on a step, staring toothless, uneaten sandwich someone gave him in his grimy hands. Other times he'll be screaming at passers by, thrusting his book of sheep and sunny hilltops at them. Once he was lashing the air with a tattered umbrella at passing cars yelling, "Fucker! Fucker! Fucker!"

Today he was bouncing up and down on one foot then the other with a broad smile while singing:

You ain't nuttin' but a hound dog!
You ain't nuttin' but a hound dog!
You ain't nuttin' but a hound dog!
You ain't nuttin' but a hound dog!

Hmmmm, seems this was the only line of the song he liked . . . or knew. "For Christ's sake Jimmy shut up!" shouted the woman working the newsstand. I walked into his cloud of foul air and said, "You ain't never caught a rabbit and you ain't no friend of mine."

He instantly switched to it:

You ain't never caught a rabbit and you ain't no friend of mine!
You ain't never caught a rabbit and you ain't no friend of mine!
You ain't never caught a rabbit and you ain't no friend of mine!
You ain't never caught a rabbit and you ain't no friend of mine!
You ain't never caught a rabbit and you ain't no friend of mine!

I stepped over to the newsstand to buy a *Philadelphia Daily News.*
The woman sneered at me, "Thanks a lot Buddy! Betcha think yer
a big help dontcha!?"

"Ah, but it's Elvis."
"No! It's Jimmy singing Elvis!"
"I disagree. I disagree completely."

If Elvis Could Hear You Now!

CALL TODAY AND LEAVE YOUR
ANONYMOUS MESSAGE TO

IT'S AS REAL
AS IF IT WERE REAL

(215) 563-3075

ELVIS HEAR ME NOW 215.563.3075	ELVIS HEAR ME NOW 215.563.3075	ELVIS HEAR ME NOW 215.563.3075	ELVIS HEAR ME NOW 215.563.3075	ELVIS HEAR ME NOW 215.563.3075	ELVIS HEAR ME NOW 215.563.3075

Hundreds called when I posted this flyer all over Philadelphia. Here are some favorites:

1. (sex kitten voice) I'll be bulimic for you Elvis if you'll be bulimic for me.

2. Hi, Elvis? Hi, I just wanted to say that I believe if they had Prozac back in your time it could've helped you . . . you know, be happier and not do all those drugs and stuff. I'm on Prozac, it is wonderful! I could be the Prozac Poster Girl! Well, anyway, yay Prozac! And yay Elvis!

3. Hi, wow, what a message. Yeah, I saw your flyer—I'm a tarot card reader near South Street. Your flyer is really eye-catching, there were actually several people hovered around it when I first noticed it. I'd like to talk to you about a trade. You help me create a good flyer for my tarot cards and I'll give you a few readings. That's why I called, I'm not an Elvis fan . . . but . . . I do have a friend who channels Elvis. She's not a fan either, you know, you don't always get to choose who you channel. Yeah, she'll be sitting there combing her hair, and, WHAM! He's there! She called me up recently to tell me He says I'm going to win the lottery. So, I'm playing the lottery, but until then I need a good flyer to get some tarot clients.

4. Most people think Elvis Presley did a whole bunch of drugs and drinking and stuff like that, and eventually died of that. But what actually happened was he mastered the art of invisibility. The whole drug thing was a big front. He was actually experimenting with raising and lowering his vibration, and he walks among us still.

5. Eat me Elvis! But I'm a lesbian, so, you can't! Unless K.D. Lang is really you!

6. Hi . . . ah . . . Elvis? I, um, used to work in a bookstore. My boss—he's such an asshole!—was such a prick when your biography *Last Train To Memphis* came out. He was always making jokes. I still fucking hate him! But, um, anyway, I wanted to buy the book for Christmas gifts anyway, so, on my boss's day off I bought all 23 copies on the shelves. He was shocked it sold out, and stopped his stupid jokes. Yeah, that showed him!

7. Elvis is dead! Get a fucking life!

8. (strange, sexless voice) Hey there, ah, this is Elvis Presley. I just want to say I appreciate what you're doing . . . and ah . . . keep the faith.

9. (whiny, sex-starved voice) Elvis!? Elvis!? You didn't show up again! I'm so disappointed! I waited for five hours! Where were you!? Elvis!? Elvis!? ELVIIIIIIIIIIIIIIIIIIIIIIIIIIIIIIIIIIIIIIIIIIIIIIIIIIIIIIIIIS!?

10. Elvis, my name is Madelaine, um, I'm your illegitimate child, so, please send money or presents to 512 South 3rd Street. My birthday's coming up soon, please don't forget, Dad.

11. I'm eating a cosmic sandwich right now and Elvis is inside it.

12. Hi. Hi Elvis. My mother and I saw you in Philadelphia on May 28th, 1977. It was so beautiful. A few months later we were watching the news and . . . heard you had died. We just hugged each other and cried and cried. (she takes a deep breath) I was so lucky I got to see you Elvis . . . the last time you came to Philly. You were so great, you were really really great. My mother and I talked for the longest time about that concert while she was in the hospital. It gave her strength. Me too, gives me strength too. I love you Elvis. You have changed so many of us . . . forever. Thank you, you dear dear man.

13. It is a little known fact that when Elvis became acquainted with someone he would often give them a small book entitled *The Voice of the Silence* by the famous theosophist H.P. Blavatsky.

14. Oh man, I couldn't wait another day, not participating in the Great Vibe. CA, this is your friend Buck Downs, I'm calling to leave you a message because somebody told me yesterday in rather substantial detail about the two times in Elvis's life when he was so enamored by the works of Samuel Beckett that he actually engaged in a correspondence with the author. And I thought you would find that to be a great piece of information to add to your word hoard. I hope you're having a great day, I'll talk to you another time.

15. I was wondering if, when Elvis shuffled off this mortal coil, if that was a special shuffle dance step? Was he doing the shuffle? You know, the "Two Street Shuffle"?

"The way to final freedom is within thy SELF."
—H.P. Blavatsky, from *The Voice of the Silence*

Dear Elvis,

I work in a gay and lesbian bookstore in Philadelphia. There's a six-and-a-half-foot lesbian who shops here who looks like a cross between You and Golda Meir. She was flattered upon hearing this comparison. She's invited me to play golf with her—she lives for golf! I think I'll go, just to see the old men react when she screams and bellows while swinging her club.

That's all for now.

From your most faithful fag,
CAConrad

p.s. Did you know there are no lesbian romance titles that begin with the letter R? Sometimes it makes me sad as a round dog caught in a tidal flush (as my Gramma would say). But sometimes I'm elated for the possibilities of R in the realm of women who love women. If You were a woman Elvis, You would be a lesbian no doubt, and would no doubt understand. Wish You had lived to do a duet with K.D. Lang.

"The quavering, sensual voice of Elvis Presley is coming from the jukebox in lonesome, sad, sustained, orgasmic moans."

—John Rechy, from *City of Night*

(Elvis in everyone)

my mother dropped cigarettes . . . rose up cigarettes
in hand . . . and for . . . a moment . . . looked like Elvis . . .
breathe in in in . . . mother "What the HELL are ya
lookin' at!" (my beautiful Elvis mother)

Norberto stepped from shower . . . dripping his . . .
and for a second. . . looked like Elvis

(my boss at the gay bookstore)

(the big lesbian golfer)

(the president especially his wife)

(each of Steven's five dogs)

(Elvis Elvis everywhere look at my fingers look at yours)

(someone hands me a book about . . . stigmata . . .
Mary . . . children see Mary on a hill . . . well I saw Elvis
combing his homeless beard with his fingers
on a steam vent today O yes I did!)

Elvis does not beat eggs.
He gently separates them,
reunites them,
separates them,
reunites them,
until quietly
folded together.

At a pagan gathering, I'm having martinis with Rose by the White
Trash Coven's Elvis Altar when a naked man with a goat on a leash
says hello and drops on all fours to worship Elvis.

The goat promptly mounts him and fucks his ass, bell around his
neck, *clang clang clang.*

It all happened so quickly, the goat came up his ass with a grunt
and they were on their way.

We didn't know what to say. We hadn't prepared for the Goatman's
visit.

Rose threw her martini back and opened a new bottle of gin
BECAUSE EVEN IF someone had said a man was going to get
fucked by a goat at the Elvis Altar there's still no way to prepare,
you simply *cannot prepare*!

ME: If Elvis drifted down to earth for your birthday to grant your ultimate sexual request, and He opened His case of angelic genitalia selection, would you prefer your Elvis with pussy, cock, both, or neither?

NAIL: I'm a lesbian! A pussy of course! How about you?

ME: Neither! I want His genitals to be a hand holding out to me a delicious butterscotch ice cream cone.

NORBERTO: Do you think people know when you're naked on the phone?

ME: Hmmmmm. I always think Elvis looks down and sees me naked. It's okay. I like that.

NORBERTO: Why do you bring him up? Why do you always bring him up!? So annoying!

*N*orberto gave me a card of Elvis dressed in gold lame. He wrote, "I love you so much I don't mind sharing you with the King!" I carried the card of my two favorite men all day. At work I counted the daily receipts, put the money in a bag for the bank. At the last minute I put the golden Elvis card in the bag, with the money, for the walk, the, walk, in, the, sun. The money rubbed Elvis. Elvis rubbed the money, the bag rubbed my thigh. Money and rubbing, Elvis and rubbing. Elvis, for you this small loan, though the money isn't mine. Money made in the gay bookstore, money made of Gertrude Stein, Stephen Jonas, Eileen Myles, Allen Ginsberg, rubbing you Elvis, rubbing you to shine! Then the teller took the money away. But the card glowed, brighter, yes brighter. "This is my new golden Elvis card," I held it for the teller to see. Her eyes widened, like she was looking at a crazy person, "Oh, yeah, I see, hm, that's very nice." I had the golden Elvis card of my two favorite men! Yes, weaving through Philadelphia, drunk on brotherly love.

• PRISCILLA PRESLEY'S MEMOIR •
ELVIS AND ME AS DIVINATION

No one absorbed the true power of Elvis more than the Queen herself, Priscilla. Try this at home: Take a question, any question your life has to offer. Open and close the book (*Elvis and Me*, 1986 Berkley paperback edition) nine times with eyes closed, concentrating on your question, and you will find your answer somewhere on the ninth opening.

Examples:

QUESTION: Elvis, can you hear me through the sheath of sonic jet fuel mist?
ANSWER: (p. 113) Elvis began calling me almost immediately, and we'd talk for hours.

QUESTION: Elvis, should I let Norberto cook me his famous marijuana burrito?
ANSWER: (p. 106) I was in such a state of ecstasy that I didn't notice what I was drinking: four double screwdrivers, all drunk through a straw.

QUESTION: Elvis, is Norberto more in love with his wife than he is with me?
ANSWER: (p. 168) I wanted to believe him, but I couldn't help noticing the national gossip magazines and the headlines about the torrid affair on the set of *Viva Las Vegas.*

QUESTION: Elvis, Norberto says I'm too weird to go out in public with him. What do you feel?

ANSWER: (p. 212) Night after night he kept his makeup and the turban on all through dinner and up until bedtime.

QUESTION: Elvis, if I surrender into my tenderness . . . for good . . . how would I survive the world?

ANSWER: (p. 215) He was convinced, and nearly had us convinced, that there were energy waves so powerful they caused the stars to glide through the universe.

QUESTION: Elvis, I'm tired of Norberto spitting overhead and catching it again in his mouth . . . actually Elvis, I'm tired of this relationship altogether. What the hell do I do?

ANSWER: (p. 162) Wearing his football helmet and his big furry Eskimo coat, Elvis proceeded, as his entourage cheered him on, to bring down the house and set it afire.

QUESTION: Elvis, am I ready to give up my Elizabeth-Taylor-chocolate-dipped-french-fry lifestyle?

ANSWER: (p. 286) Elvis was never much of a letter writer, but he now wrote President Nixon a letter explaining how he could assist the youth of today in getting off drugs.

QUESTION: Elvis, how do I explain the footprints on the refrigerator door to my landlord?

ANSWER: (p. 216) "Do you see them?" said Elvis, looking intently at the course. "See what?" I asked, ready to hear anything. "The angels, out there."

QUESTION: Elvis, why did you die when you did?
ANSWER: (p. 210) It was this kind of higher state of consciousness that Elvis was hoping to achieve.

QUESTION: Elvis, I've had many dreams of you, but I'm confused by the messages.
ANSWER: (p. 204) He asked Larry why, out of all the people in the universe, he had been chosen to influence so many millions of souls.

QUESTION: Elvis, how am I doing writing *Advanced ELVIS Course?*
ANSWER: (p. 89) I'd never played blackjack before, but after a few hands, Elvis thought I had the hang of it.

• ANIMATION FAMILY WITH •
ELVIS EVERYDAY

Every morning Timmy pleads with our Mama not to draw him a penis. "You're a boy Timmy, shut up! Just because you're a cartoon, doesn't mean you get what you want!" Elvis is never drawn until noon, gives us a chance to have some peace and quiet. First we draw the yard real pretty, lots of flowers, Mama draws flowers the prettiest. Elvis is drawn sitting on a picnic blanket with freshly drawn meatloaf sandwiches, mmm mm! Sure enough, Elvis will be singing us a song, telling jokes, and being particularly kind to Mama, when suddenly Timmy stalks onto the scene in a freshly drawn wig and evening gown to take Elvis's breath away. That Timmy ruins it every damn time! Elvis sings a love song to Timmy, stops half way through, takes Timmy in his arms and makes love to him right there on top of the meatloaf sandwiches every damn time! We busy ourselves drawing walls around their lusty, moaning bodies, "Hurry!" Mama yells, "Hurry, draw faster! I don't want to see this! That boy of mine takes Elvis from us every time! I swear, and I know I've threatened this a thousand times before, but tomorrow I will draw Timmy on horseback galloping away for the day!"

After reading several pieces from *Advanced ELVIS Course* **for an** audience at a Philadelphia coffee house, I am approached by the christian poet Helen.

HELEN: (curled lip, mouth full of bitter) I heard your Elvis stories!

ME: Yeah?

HELEN: Yeah. I think it's cultish, this Elvis stuff.

ME: Hm. The word cult has gotten a bad name.

HELEN: Yeah! And for good reason!

ME: Do you think so?

HELEN: Do I think so!? Yes I think so!

ME: Wasn't christianity a cult once?

HELEN: What!? Are you kidding!? The son of god part of a cult!?

ME: Sure, imagine, a small group of zealous believers in the 1st century AD, lurking around, preaching to anyone who'll listen.

HELEN: Christianity is not and never was a cult!

ME: I bet if you went back in time and asked anyone who didn't believe, I bet they'd think so.

HELEN: Oh, you are! Oh! I am praying for you CAConrad!

ME: Seriously though, don't you believe the only difference between a cult and a religion is the size of the congregation?

HELEN: I'm praying for you!

ME: Oh. Well, I guess that means the conversation is over then?

HELEN: I'm praying! I'm praying!

• DREAM OF WATCHING JOHNNY CARSON •
INTERVIEW ELVIS ON TV

Johnny tells a joke and everyone laughs. Elvis tells a joke and everyone laughs harder because everyone loves Elvis more.

JOHNNY: So, Elvis, tell us what you think of Madonna.

ELVIS: Oh, I think she's got some real good tunes, and ah, she has a sweet pair of tits.

JOHNNY: She sure is a beauty.

ELVIS: Yeah, yeah, I wouldn't mind sticking my pencil in her knish.

JOHNNY: Knish!? Are you, ah, Jewish?

ELVIS: Yeah well, you know, I thought I'd give it a try, I mean, hey it can't hurt, right?

JOHNNY: O! Well, sure, sure. Um, MAZEL TOV to ya Elvis!

ELVIS: Yeah, mazel tov Johnny, mazel tov.

> (Elvis says he has a surprise phone call to make. The TV
> audience gets real quiet while he dials. My phone rings,
>   it's probably Michelle calling to say Elvis is on TV.)

ME: (never taking my eyes off TV) Hello?

ELVIS: Hi, is this Conrad in Philadelphia?

ME: (silent . . . can't believe it's true . . . but I see him on TV . . . hear him and see him . . . talking to me)

ELVIS: Is this Conrad?

ME: Oh, ah, hello, Elvis, yes Elvis, it's me, it's Conrad, ah, hi.

ELVIS: (low & sexy) You've been a bad boy. Mmmm. Haven't you?

ME: Oh, I mean no, no Elvis.

ELVIS: You're lying. Mmmm. You want to suck my cock, don't you, hm? Don't you boy?

(the audience oooooooos and aaahs)

ME: Me, um, I, I, ah—

ELVIS: Yeah, oooo, yeah, you'd like that wouldn't you? Hm? My big fat cock in your mouth, hm? Yeah, yeah.

ME: (I black out)

ELVIS: (to Johnny) I don't know where he went.

JOHNNY: My goodness Elvis, I think you put him in a coma. (the audience laughs)

" . . . Elvis's body of musical work"

"Did you say Elvis's body was musical work?"

"OF!"

"Oh . . . well . . . I say was."

Interview with the author of *Advanced ELVIS Course*

ME: Have you ever jerked off while fantasizing about Elvis?

ME: I don't jerk off.

ME: Yeah, right. Well, have you ever fantasized about Elvis while making love to someone?

ME: Not "to" someone, it's "with." And there's no need to fantasize. Ever since Elvis took the stage in the late 1950s, every man has genetically enterprised in actual time/flesh, different aspects of Elvis to profit from the enormous burden of attraction he instilled upon the species. Elvis is always in bed with you, even in most cases of lesbian sex.

ME: What about Norberto?

ME: The reason my relationship with Norberto has lasted as long as it has is due to the enormous number of attributes of Elvis he has absorbed.

ME: Does he know this?

ME: No, most men have absorbed these qualities on a subconscious level. It's those who are aware of the Elvis they have adopted in their love-making that have a particular flair for the type of sexual spontaneity which will ultimately move that soul forward to a higher frequency.

ME: How do we discover a lover's Elvis aspects, and how do we let them know?

ME: Well, telling them about it runs the risk of sounding insane. What I've done to move forward spiritually with my lover—because that is, hopefully, the goal—is play Elvis music while we're in bed. What this does is connect his absorbed Elvis aspects with the vibration of Elvis's actual vibrato which put those absorbed aspects in him in the first place. Almost instantly you will notice a connection, a heightened awareness in the various movements to the opera of your love-making.

ME: What songs do you recommend?

ME: It's good to experiment. Each soul has fused with a different combination of Elvis aspects which best aids their awareness and eventual progression. I've found Norberto and I move forward as bonded souls with such songs as "Kentucky Rain," "All Shook Up," "Surrender," and particularly the entire soundtrack to *Viva Las Vegas*. Norberto has the largest variety of Elvis aspects of any man I've ever known. He's an advanced soul who is allowing himself to press forward faster with me.

ME: Even though he's married already?

ME: His wife is not aware of his Elvis aspects. It's clear he experiences a different state of consciousness when he's with me. And besides, Norberto and I have much karma to run our fingers through by aligning our Elvis aspects.

ME: What about the songs? Is it the words?

ME: The surface content of the songs has some effect, yes, but it's really the actual sound wave itself, still hidden to the optic nerve of the human eye in our present state of physical evolution on earth. The sound waves of Elvis carry deeply buried, deeply important signals which adjust, readjust, align, and ultimately raise the source of light in the tissue, fusing the purpose of the tissue with the purpose of the soul, which came to earth encoded for the journey of a life.

ME: Does the orgasm play a role in the sexual/spiritual process?

ME: The orgasm is a reward on the physical plane only. The orgasm does interrupt, and often undo much of the Elvis aspect alignment, which means prolonged love-making is much preferred to ensure that a new level of raised frequency and light is reached. I find if it's too quick, an orgasm can actually reverse the achieved levels of previous Elvis aspect love-making. But then again, we can't spend all day in bed.

ME: The world would probably be a better place though.

ME: Oh yes, I'm convinced the rhythm of worldwide love-making for a solid 24 hours would shudder the planet to its core, causing a planetary orgasm which would connect us with our true Elvis aspects right off the physical plane for good.

Elvis, today Michelle and I were driving on 95 South and we saw the Golden Potato Masher . . . we wanted you to know . . . because we love you . . . it feels good . . . we hear your songs MY GOD Elvis we hear you

• TWO OF THE MOST FAMOUS •
TWO SYLLABLE NAMES

Dreamt I wrote E-L-V-I-S, held it to the mirror and it read
K-A-F-K-A. It was the possibilities that woke me! The possibilities!
There's plenty of room for Graceland in Prague! Elvis would have
made the most handsome Gregor Samsa in the musical version of
The Metamorphosis. A full-body insect costume with six hairy legs,
and that beautiful face of sideburns, alone in his room with a plate
of spoiled potato salad, singing "I Got a Feelin' in My Body."

Dreamt I was looking at a painting titled "Night Club Bouncer." Elvis was on a tiny, pedestal-like stage dressed in a glittering white suit with cape, arms stretched overhead. The entire audience was hundreds of tiny Kafkas, staring with those wounded, sexy eyes. The bouncer was an angry Kafka, dragging a screaming Kafka out the door. Kafka was throwing himself out of the Elvis concert! But there were still hundreds of Kafkas left inside, watching Elvis with wounded, sexy eyes.

quoth the raven

"OPIUM!"

quoth the canary

"DEXEDRINE!"

Edgar **Elvis**
Allan **Aaron**
Poe **Presley**

Another goddamned fucking yuppie car almost ran me down today!
I was furious! Furious! Then an old pick-up truck stopped at a red light, Elvis on the radio singing:

> *So my darling surrender,*
> *All your love so warm and tender*
> *Let me hold you in my arms dear,*
> *While the moon shines bright above . . .*

Ooooh, thank you Elvis. I relaxed. Really really relaxed. Sky overhead turning the jar lid of release. Relaxed, relaxed, my sphincter opened its baby bird mouth, hungry, but relaxed . . . thank you King.

 caught my soul in the air like a rose between His teeth!

Walking down 7th & Chestnut, Philadelphia.

ME: (waving wildly) Hey Tyrone! How ya doin'!?

TYRONE: Hey Conrad man! This is Shaylee.

ME: Nice to meet you Shaylee.

SHAYLEE: Nice to meet you Conrad.

ME: Tyrone, why's your umbrella up? It's not raining man.

TYRONE: Not in your world maybe.

SHAYLEE: He's hiding from God.

ME: Oh . . . You still have your Elvis button I see.

TYRONE: (breaks into song) "KNOCK! And the door shall be opened!"

SHAYLEE: "SEEK! And you will find!"

TYRONE: "ASK! And you'll be given"

ME: "The KEY to this heart of mine!"

TYRONE: Welcome to my world man! Welcome to my world!

ME: What are you two up to today?

SHAYLEE: Watchin' all the normal people. Look at him over there in the suit! So normal it's a sin!

TYRONE: Brother needs to eat a little garbage! Garbage will swing a man wide open!

One of my favorite vices is littering in wealthy neighborhoods. For days I save litter for the million dollar houses and condominiums: candy wrappers, wads of dirty tissues, used condoms, mayonnaise jars nearly licked clean, expired Atlantic City casino coupons.

I kiss my picture of Elvis and promise Him I will NEVER litter in the neighborhoods of the poor! NEVER!

I can hear Him answer, "LET THE RICH MAN KNOW HIS TRUE WORTH! LET HIM SEE THE CONDITION OF HIS SOUL ON THE STREETS OUTSIDE HIS HOME!"

I promise Elvis, *I will, I will!*

Without violence there is conversation in my mother's house. I teach two year-old Sydney "Elvis! Elvis! Elvis! Elvis!" Gramma is very sick.

ME: (sitting next to her bed) What did you dream last night Gramma?

GRAMMA: Oh, a woman I don't know was gettin' ready for Halloween.

ME: Halloween Gramma?

GRAMMA: Yeah! And I told her I wasn't helping her!

SYDNEY: Elvis! Elvis! Elvis! Elvis!

GRAMMA: Yeah! Elvis! Elvis! Elvis! Elvis! That's right kiddo!

*I*ris Murdoch is dead. Died yesterday, exactly one month after the birthday of our Elvis. Cut her obituary from the *Philadelphia Inquirer.* Weather report alongside. Cut around it, map of USA with temperatures and storm fronts. Gonna frame obituary/weather report. As a young woman, she was denied scholarship in USA for her communist background. New York was fifty-four degrees of forgiveness yesterday. Cold front close behind.

"I would give my life, I think, more willingly than I would give my mind."
—Iris Murdoch, from *An Accidental Man*

Dreamt our teacher waited on the ground while we ten-year-olds
climbed the tree at midnight with pocket telescopes. The climbing
was swift monkey action. We secretly floated the last few feet,
never telling the teacher we could hover, just above the treetop.
We eagerly viewed a newly discovered constellation called Jason
& Medea. We knew it was really Graceland, the dense twinkling
cluster of stars in the foreground the entrance gate, and we knew
the twinkling was the gate opening and closing across the black
sky for lost souls seeking refuge.

"Do you feel it open and close?"

"Yes, do you feel the pull?"

"We come spinning out of nothingness, scattering stars like dust."
—Rumi

• USED BOOKSTORE IN PHILADELPHIA •
SMELLING SUSPICIOUSLY LIKE A
VERY CLEAN WOMAN PREGNANT
WITH A LAWYER

ME: Excuse me? Where do you keep your Elvis books?

CLERK: Well, um, we don't have an Elvis section. I mean . . . you might want to check the Biography section.

ME: You mean he's not in Spirituality?

CLERK: Ah, well. Um . . . should he be?

If I stand still long enough I would be a place
and no one wants to visit a place that's been a man too long
Elvis once stood still for five minutes in downtown Memphis
stood still in such a way no one knew how to get there

Dreamt I was ice skating in Rockefeller Center. Someone yelled "Elvis! The ghost of Elvis! Look!" There He was, driving a ghost snowmobile around the ice rink. He aimed the ghost snowmobile at a woman and charged her! She screamed, but He drove through her, leaving her tottering in place. She began laughing with a deep, booming cough-laugh, laughing higher and higher till she was crying from laughing so hard. He drove through everybody on the rink, each frightened and screaming at first, then filling with the same deep laughter. Finally He came at me. Those few seconds as He approached are forever imprinted in my memory: The gleaming smile, the intent in the brow, determined to do what He must, and the white jump suit, fringe flapping those daring, handsome sideburns! As the ghost of Elvis on His ghost snowmobile passed through me I felt an instant scraping of my organs, painful, hurtful, feeling Him inside me. When I wobbled steady I could hear the harrow of dark laughter churning ever higher from deep within, up, up, up, up, and out my mouth, and I fell into the laughter with everyone else on the rink. Good stranger, we are cleansed by Him together.

"Thy shadows live and vanish; that which in thee shall live for ever, that which in thee knows, for it is knowledge, is not of fleeting life: it is the Man that was, that is, and will be, for whom the hour shall never strike."

— H.P. Blavatsky, from *The Voice of the Silence*

Geek hair, geek eyes, glasses, true geek mouth uncovered by soundlings, oh Dave. Date with dreamy nerd Dave tonight, and he likes Elvis which is a plus. Well, he tolerates Elvis, I shouldn't exaggerate.

ME: I have an Elvis heart.

DAVE: What's that, a heart of bacon grease and narcotics?

ME: HEY! You said you LIKE Elvis!

DAVE: I said I tolerate Elvis, let's not exaggerate.

Trying to read the poem "How I Lost My Notebook" by Eileen Myles
in coffee shop the man and woman behind me start talking about
Elvis and at first it's hard to concentrate then pretty soon all the lines
of the poem can't compete which says nothing about Eileen Myles
who has never faltered my attentions but Elvis Elvis I hear Elvis and
I'd stop reading even a tear-swept letter from my mother:

Quietly wishing I
had testicles

Elvis part of that? I mean

Elvis concert my mom saw.

Oh yeah? Wow. I'm not a fan though

Yeah, well I am.

lost three

I didn't know that.

Sure, Elvis is an American emblem!

what were the
other two

Well . . . sure . . . I guess so.

Elvis is a hero for Working Class America.

I wouldn't go that far.

a heaving

Why not? I certainly believe it's so.

hole & the
second

I don't know. I guess I think Elvis just gets way too much
attention.

roommate
observed

Ah, EXCUSE ME, but, the man built BRIDGES!

Huh?

Bridges between the north and the south.

me, it

Bridges between blacks and whites.

slipping

How so?

out

By bringing black music into mainstream

plop

American culture.

Oh. I never thought of that.

Elvis is a hero.

Okay, okay.

He's a fucking hero!

Elvis didn't know why His foot wore a black veil to be away from the world. People asked Him, "Whose foot is that with the veil?" Embarrassed, He'd say "I don't know I don't know!" One day a passing truck blew the veil away. Startled, they stared at one another. "It is good my foot," He said, "you will have a new life." Next morning His foot was wearing a pink and yellow suit with gold and silver buttons.

" . . . perhaps the museum of his memory."

—Chris Marker, from *La Jetée*

When I was twelve I understood the love of Elvis in ways impalpable to others. Approaching a stop sign on my bicycle I would exalt the truth of His Love, "I know you love me and I can ride through the stop sign without looking!"

Flying through the intersection with closed eyes FREE! AND! LOVE!

HONK-HONK! "You almost got run the fuck over you stupid fucking kid!"

Ah, almost meant He was there for me. He can, like no one, keep death at bay. It's moments like this when I wish Elvis had molested me instead of the creepy neighbor guy.

All the worst things could be better with His divine hillbilly hands.

Spell Mary Magdalin's last name: Magdelain? Magdalen? Dictionary is no good. Could skim the New Testament looking for her. No thanks. I call my good friend Maria with twelve years of Catholic school under her belt: Saints, confessions, when to light candles, when to eat fish, when to kneel, how to kneel. Should your lips touch priesty fingers offering communion wafers? There's a priest downtown whose fingers are very suckable! Yummmmmmm! Priesty-priesty! Maria knows the answers. Only need to know how to spell Magdilan though. Left a message on her machine. Just waiting now. My finishing touches on *Advanced ELVIS Course.* Need the spelling of our sacred whore.